LAURE

D0193735

Hereafter

What happens after Death?
DAVID WINTER

Harold Shaw Publishers
and
The Christian Book Promotion Trust
Wheaton, Illinois

*Copyright © 1972 by David Winter
ISBN 0-440-16003-9
Harold Shaw Publishers edition 1973
published by special arrangement
with Hodder and Stoughton Ltd., London.*

*ISBN 0-87788-341-6
Library of Congress catalog card
number 72-94097*

6th printing, August 1976

Printed in the United States of America

CONTENTS

INTRODUCTION

"There is darkness without, and when I die there will be darkness within. There is no splendour, no vastness anywhere; only triviality for a moment, and then nothing." So wrote Bertrand Russell before his death, and in two sentences he captured what many, many people today feel about life, and death.

As man has reached out into space, and probed inward to the mysteries of the human mind and body, he has fallen victim to his own cleverness. In trying to become god, he has found himself simply to be a cog in a machine. In trying to defeat death, he has given it its greatest victory. Perhaps for the first time in human history we have a whole civilization that believes there is nothing beyond death but darkness . . . and the void of nothingness.

This is reflected in current popular attitudes. Various opinion polls, in Europe as well as the U.S.A., have shown that a substantial minority rejects the idea of life after death in any shape or form. And this minority is growing. Even "religious" people, churchgoers of all denominations, are among those who either check the "don't know" blank on the questionnaire or say definitely that they do not believe in life after death. Certainly among my own circle of Christian friends there are few who believe it with any degree of conviction.

Perhaps this erosion of an old belief has helped to create our modern obsession with death. Not that people talk about it all the time: quite the contrary. They studiously refuse to consider it. But its very absence is the sign of its power over us. Because we are afraid of death we try to ignore it. Rosalind Heywood tells of a distinguished critic who refused to review a scholarly book weighing the evidence for survival, on the ground that even if it contained waterproof evidence his readers would not be interested. A newspaper editor was so shocked by the idea of such a book that he vowed to censor any account of such proof in his paper. Miss Heywood asked a Freudian analyst for his view of their attitude. His reply: these people were simply repressing their own fear of death by refusing to consider it.

Most of those who now reject the idea of "survival" after death have been consciously or subconsciously influenced by the materialism of this century, and by materialistic science. They believe —often simply on hearsay or general impression— that "science" (whatever that is) has "disproved" (whatever that means) the idea of "immortality." They may have heard the vivid phrase of philosopher Gilbert Ryle, "There is no ghost in the human machine." Certainly the spectacular advance of space science and of knowledge about the universe has undermined the faith of those who believed in a crudely literal "heaven" "above the bright blue sky." We all know that above the bright blue sky is a lot more sky, and then even more: millions of light years of it.

Radio telescopes have probed into the far reaches of space, and have found no pearly gates; no New Jerusalems. Obviously, many of the old ideas are wrong at the factual, scientific level. And with those superstitious and pseudo-biblical myths has gone the whole concept of a life beyond this life, entered through a door we call death.

The object of this book is to help to bring back again the validity of immortality; to show that, properly understood, there is nothing impossible, nothing even unlikely about "life after death;" that many modern discoveries and insights make it even *easier* for us to accept immortality now, than it could have been for our grandparents. In the process of exploring this subject I hope to show that to reject the idea of life after death is unreasonable prejudice, requiring the kind of firmly closed mind formerly attributed to Christians who believed in it.

Life beyond death is, I believe, an essential part of the good news that God revealed in Jesus

Christ. It is a part of the Christian faith that modern man needs almost more than any other; a belief that transforms his whole attitude to life, and to death. I believe that ordinary men and women have totally misunderstood what "science" says and does not say in this area, and that a priceless element of the good life has been stolen from them without their realizing it.

"There is no death, but the people do not believe it." So J. Paterson Smyth wrote in his classic tract *The Gospel of the Hereafter* sixty years ago.[1] There is no "darkness," no empty void, beyond. There is no end to the progress of human personality, because there is no end to God, who is its fixed point. For the Christian believer there is no need to fear. That is the Christian position, and it is one which can bear any examination. I do not say that any of us can prove that there is life after death but I would claim that anyone who comes without prejudice to the evidence will at least have to agree with a famous brain specialist, Sir John Eccles, who said "I cannot believe that the gift of conscious experience has no further future, no possibility of another existence under some other intangible conditions. At least I would maintain that this possibility of a future existence cannot be denied on scientific grounds."[2]

The time has come, surely, to reinstate the full Christian doctrine of eternal life to the high place it deserves, in our pulpits, on our lips, and in our hearts. This book is simply an attempt to provoke twentieth-century people into looking again at something that has meant so much to past generations, and has been needlessly and arbitrarily rejected by the very age that needs it most.

notes.

[1] *Hodder.*

[2] *Quoted in the symposium* Man's Concern with Death, *Hodder, 1968.*

MODERN MAN LOOKS AT DEATH

The little girl splashed through a puddle and got mud on her socks. After examining it with a critical eye she asked her mother, "What's mud for?"

Mother searched rapidly for a convincing answer, and found it. "For making bricks, dear."

"What are bricks for?"

"Making houses, dear."

"What are houses for?"

"People."

The little girl only paused for a second, and then asked the question to which her mother had no reply.

"And what are people for?"

It is the question modern man hides from, and yet without it, all his other questions and all his elaborate answers to them are so much whistling in the dark.

Previous generations, which had no idea at all how magnetism worked, or how radio waves operated, had satisfying and consistent answers to the question of the nature and destiny of man. Part of our modern dilemma is that we have found out *how* but we have forgotten *why*.

Man's life, in terms of cosmic time, is the mere spitting of a tiny spark in the darkness, so brief that it can hardly be seen. And yet these brief human lives have achieved so much, in terms of art and beauty, of creativity and science. It is hard to accept that man's destiny is to turn on the surface of this tiny planet. Indeed, until the present day, the great majority of men have believed that his destiny lay far beyond it, in some future life beyond physical death.

But we have lost that belief, regarding it as too naïve, too unscientific for our more sophisticated age. And with it we have lost a whole dimension of life. Man has reached out to the stars, but shackled his feet to time and space.

It seems a long way from the days when the ambition of many a Christian was to "make a good death," to his modern counterpart who spends his life trying to postpone it and hoping that he will meet it suddenly and unawares. We speak with envy of the man or woman instantly taken away by a sudden heart attack: he "knew nothing about it," it was "mercifully swift." All sorts of conspiracies are indulged in to keep from the dying person a knowledge of his true condition, and when he finally dies enormous precautions are taken to ensure that his passing upsets or disturbs as few people as possible. As

a result, most Americans are deprived of a
healthy confrontation with the reality of death.
The conditioning which denies death also denies personal grief and prevents the emotional
release which true grieving brings. The dead—
who were a source of inspiration and comfort
to our forefathers—are frankly an embarrassment to us. They remind us of our own mortality, and we prefer to think ourselves immortal.

It is a strange fact that many an adult American has never actually seen anybody die. When
we consider that over fifty thousand people die
in the United States every week, we see how ef-
fectively we have curtained ourselves off from
reality. Death happens to everyone, once in every
seventy years or so. We are all aware of this, but
by some trick of self-deception what we are really
thinking is that *death happens to everyone else*.

In an age when almost everybody believed that
"it is appointed for men to die once, and after
that comes judgement."[1] this belief moulded a
man's life. He lived with one eye on eternity. This
was by no means a morbid obsession. It led to
faith rather than fear. Far from being terrified of
death, he prepared for it all his days and faced it
not only as the completion of a life well lived but
as the transition to a new life. Modern man, with
his arid materialism, is more worried by death,
more anxious about what he sees as his extinction
when it happens, and less confident of his ability
to cope with it either in prospect or in the event.

And that this is a real loss there can be no doubt. Modern medicine has found answers to most physical illnesses, but has substantially failed to find an answer to the black plague of the twentieth century, mental illness. The so-called stress diseases, anxiety, depression and other neuroses, literally plague the brash, affluent men and women of North America and Western Europe. And behind much of it lies our suppressed—even, perhaps, subconscious—fear of death.

It is this suppression of fear that is so dangerous. It makes us unwilling to face facts. It makes nonsense of our claims to be "Christian." And it paralyzes our enjoyment of life. The New Testament describes it in disturbingly accurate words: "through fear of death ... subject to lifelong bondage."[2]

But it was precisely in order to release men from this "lifelong bondage" that Christ came to earth. It is tragic that at the moment when we really need it, most of us have lost our hold on this part of the Christian "good news." The apostle Paul could taunt the specter, death: "Where is your sting ... where is your victory?" That requires a degree of confidence, of faith, that most of us simply cannot command. Even in our churches we seldom raise the subject, let alone dispose of the specter. Death haunts our days and disturbs our nights, when in fact he is a crippled and disabled foe whose days are numbered.

We have turned to substitute answers—to spiritualism, with its empty message of ghosts and twilight; to reincarnation, with its backbreaking emphasis on human effort and merit-earning; or to hedonism, calling us to "eat, drink and be (superficially) merry," for tomorrow we go out like a light. And all the while the Christian answer, which served our fathers so well, lies ignored or disbelieved, like a priceless heirloom disintegrating in the attic.

But of course, it is still believed, and strongly believed, by a significant number of people, and for many of us it remains the *only* consistent and satisfying theory available.

The Christian doctrine of life beyond death meets the main criteria for a sound working hypothesis: it fits the known evidence, it provides a satisfactory answer to the problem posed, and it stands without either internal or external contradiction. Rightly understood, it is a magnificently strong and consistent "system." In preparing this book, for example, I have not at any point been logically embarrassed by any detail of the Christian doctrine of resurrection, nor have I found any point at which this doctrine raised problems of inconsistency or contradiction.

It ought to be said, of course, that this only applies to the Christian concept of life beyond death in its full, biblical form. When parts of it are compromised, inner inconsistencies begin to appear. This is where the churches have found so much embarrassment over the whole subject of life beyond death. In an attempt to make their traditional doctrines more palatable to naturalistic man, they have only succeeded in making them totally indigestible.

As will become obvious, I am not advocating a wooden literalism where the Christian doctrine of the "after-life" is concerned, but simply that the basic beliefs that Christians have held since apostolic times—not the superstitions and popular myths that have become attached to them—are consistent and convincing. As far as possible I have tried to confine myself to those "basic beliefs"— what the central, orthodox, tradition of Christianity has always held, based on what the Bible clearly teaches. This is not a "catholic" or "protestant" or "evangelical" view of the matter, but what is common to all orthodox Christians. There is plenty of room for difference over the details and applications of these beliefs, but they are not central to the argument.

The remainder of this book is taken up with a point by point advocacy of the Christian doctrine of life beyond death, set in the context of modern man and his search for truth, and argued in the light of what we know about that man—his mind, his nature, his spirit, and his needs.

Paterson Smyth, in a book to which I have already referred, which provided tremendous encouragement and comfort to a war-torn and fearful generation, ended his "Foreword" with these words: "This book is a poor, imperfect attempt to put together some of the teachings of our holy religion, to help a troubled world, in the day of its necessity, to look out over the wall." And so, in a rather different but equally troubled world, is this one.

notes
[1] *Hebrews 9:27.*
[2] *Hebrews 2:15.*

2
WHAT HAPPENS WHEN I DIE?

There are many books to tell us what will happen when we leave school, get married, have a baby, or retire from work, but very few indeed to tell us what is likely to happen when an even commoner occurrence comes to us, death. Perhaps it is part of the human conspiracy of silence on the whole subject. Or perhaps it is that we feel there is really nothing to say. If what "happens" when I die is that I cease to "happen" any more, then there is little more to be said. Indeed, one of the most brilliant philosophers of the Western world, Wittgenstein, expressed this idea in intensely final terms: "As in death, too, the world does not change, but ceases. *Death is not an event in life.*"

But for the Christian, death is most emphatically an "event" in life; almost *the* event. It is part of a progress, not the end of the world. The Christian has something to say about dying which goes much further than simply seeing it as the withering away of his individual world. And what he has to say is highly relevant to every man.

Jung said that a belief in immortality had therapeutic power, because "no one can live in peace in a house that he knows is shortly to tumble about his ears." Yet so much naturalistic philosophy and popular "science" is telling modern man not so much that his house is going to tumble about his ears, but that at a future date it will suddenly cease to exist altogether, and so will the whole world in which he stands. There may be a certain nobility involved in facing that sort of destiny bravely and with dignity, but it is a comfortless concept. When the crutch of belief in immortality is knocked away, the dying man is left to cling to the material world as long as he can, and then slide into oblivion. No wonder he fights and struggles— often with very little dignity at all—to keep a hold, however tenuous, on life. No wonder he sees death as the archenemy, the final, inescapable disaster. And no wonder his life becomes more and more a feverish attempt to avoid not only death itself, but even *thinking* about death.

Yet if there is one thing psychologists and psychiatrists agree about, it is that a healthy attitude to death is absolutely essential if the last decades of life are not to become an appalling and fearful misery. The thoughts of an old person are increasingly taken up with death, and "indeed it must be so" writes Erastus Evans,[1] "if the person is to remain psychologically and spiritually healthy . . . Unless the certainty of death is taken clearly into consciousness and faced squarely, it is impossible for the old person to live the last years of life with peace and dignity." This suggests that modern attempts to ignore death are psychologically damaging, and there would appear to be evidence that this is so.

Of course, just because belief in immortality helps a man to adjust emotionally to the idea of inevitable death is no argument at all for or against the truth of immortality. We face a situation in which fewer and fewer people believe in life after death. How *are* they to be helped? Are we to *pretend* that there is survival, in order to quieten their fears and give them a few years of bogus hope? There is a new element here, and it calls in question our honesty as well as our compassion. Is there any real comfort in a lie? Can "faith" be built on deception? And in any case can we ourselves, when it is our turn to face death, set aside a life-time of scepticism and swallow a doctrine of immortality which we have rejected since adolescence?

And so the crucial question is not "Does belief in life after death help us to face death?" (it manifestly does) but "Is it true?" For modern people, shaped by the popular philosophies of the day, there is no other option. We cannot call upon a tribal tradition or an accepted folk-myth which entered our sub-conscious in childhood and has lain there dormant until required. It simply does not exist. We have to face the more difficult, more demanding but also infinitely more rewarding question, "What is the truth of the matter?" Facing that honestly may well be the preparation we need for facing death honestly. If we decide there is no life beyond, then we can grit our metaphorical teeth and prepare to face with stoical dignity the final extinction of being. But if we conclude that there *is* life beyond the grave, then the whole business of dying and death assumes a totally different perspective. There is hope: not an illusion, not an induced self-deception, not a conspiracy of friends and relatives to ease our departure, but solid, reliable, trustworthy *hope*.

What happens to my body?
So, what happens when I die? First of all, what happens to my body?

Medically, the answer is fairly simple—not as simple as it once was, but still a good deal easier than all the other answers concerning death. There are currently three competing definitions of medical death. They have been described by Dr. Henry Beecher of Harvard[2] as:

1. The moment at which irreversible destruction of brain matter, with no possibility of regaining consciousness, was conclusively determined.

2. The moment at which spontaneous heart beat could not be restored.

3. "Brain death" as established by the EEG (electroencephalogram).

In recent years there have been many cases of

recovery of people who, by older definitions, were "dead." But these are borderline instances. For the most part not only doctors but lay-people, too, know when a person, or an animal, is "dead."

Theologically, death is the disintegration of the body. "Then the dust returns to the earth as it was"—with its corollary: "and the spirit returns to God who gave it."[3] The body, deprived of "the spirit," has served its purpose. Weary and literally worn out, or brought low by disease, or struck down by accident, it "gives up the ghost" and very soon it has all but disappeared. The moment death comes, disintegration begins. It is as though nature cannot wait to complete its cycle, and recover all the chemical riches which for a lifetime have been stored in the body.

Interestingly, this process has never been regarded by human beings as a devaluation of humanity. Rather the contrary: funeral rites have served to emphasize the worth and dignity of human life. "At different times and places the dead bodies of human beings have been honored in an amazing variety of ways. They have been buried in graves or in tombs or under tumuli or inside pyramids. They have been burnt on pyres, and the ashes have been preserved in urns or have been scattered to the winds. But however diverse man's funerary rites have been, they have all had a common signification. They have signified that a human being has a dignity in virtue of his being human; that his dignity survives his death; and that therefore his dead body must not simply be treated as garbage and be thrown away like the carcass of a dead non-human creature, or like a human being's worn-out boots or clothes."[4]

So what happens to the body at death is quite simply that it changes from being a living thing to a dead one, and its physical disintegration begins. Of course, in a sense it has already begun, because all our adult lives we are "dying"; the process of deterioration, of growing old, is going on. Death is its crisis, however. We all know that, and it is best to face it, as realistically as we can. Whatever hope the Christian faith holds for the future of personality, it holds no future at all for the body in which that personality has lived on earth.

A misunderstanding (and, in one case, a mistranslation) of isolated verses in the Bible may in the past have given rise to the idea that our present physical bodies will survive death. I am thinking especially of the famous words in Job, immortalized in Handel's *Messiah*: "I know that my Redeemer lives, and that he shall stand at the latter day upon the earth; and though after my skin worms destroy this body, yet *in my flesh* shall I see God."[5] That certainly sounds quite clear: by a miracle of miracles my disintegrated body will be restored in heaven. In fact, the meaning of the Hebrew original is very unclear—so unclear that the alternate rendering of the more recent and more reliable Revised Standard Version translates the phrase in the exactly opposite sense: "After my skin has been thus destroyed, then *without my flesh* I shall see God." The concept of immortality is just as clear, but now our "survival" is not in the earth-bound body, but in another, heavenly one: and this is consistent with the main-stream of the Bible's teaching on death and resurrection.

So at death the body dies. It is discarded, with due reverence, and very soon disintegrates. This leaves the second half of that intriguing sentence in the generally pessimistic book of Ecclesiastes to consider: "And the spirit returns to God, who gave it." Here is the rub, the dividing of the ways between those who believe that death is the end of being, and those who believe it is not. Does "anything" survive death? As the body of John Jones disintegrates, does "anything" of John Jones remain? And if so, what?

The ghost in the machine
Let us clear a few preliminary hurdles first of all. For instance, there is this notion of a "ghost in the human machine," a phrase coined, or at least popularized by Gilbert Ryle. The idea behind it is that Christians and others believe that into the physical human frame God plants a soul—the "ghost in the machine"—which acts as the repository of our moral and spiritual notions, and at death leaves the body and goes back to God (or heaven, or purgatory, or whatever). Ryle and those who think with him, having caricatured the Christian view of man, then proceed to reject the carica-

ture as though it were the real thing.

In fact, so far as I know no serious Christian theologian this century has held such a crude and arbitrary view of the "soul." Biblical Christians do not subscribe to any view of human nature which divides it into mutually autonomous and independent parts. Man is a whole, a unity: body, mind, and spirit. And man in his totality, the Bible teaches, *is* (not *has* or *contains*) a soul.[6] So various experiments which have been undertaken, such as weighing a human body before and after the moment of death to see if anything is missing, if there is any weight change, are faintly ludicrous. One might as well try to weigh a sense of humor, or a feeling of depression, or a passionate love. It speaks volumes for the crude materialism of man that he should for one moment suppose that *reality* is the same thing as *weight or volume*. Christians do not believe that there is a "ghost in the machine," because they do not believe that man is a machine. He is a human being, physically an animal, spiritually "little less than God."[7] The whole person is more than simply his physique, and may well survive the death of his outward form, without being described as a "ghost." But we shall return to that later.

Our second hurdle is that the area of life beyond is an area of faith. We can test our beliefs against known facts, but short of dying ourselves we shall never be able to "prove" them. What I want to do is to state the Christian view (as I understand it) and then, in later chapters, to test that view as rigorously as I can in order to demonstrate its consistency and rationality. No one can do more than that, honestly; and no one can fairly ask for more than that, either.

What is man?

The third hurdle is really a very big one, and concerns the nature of man. If we are to ask what happens to John Jones when he dies, then we need to be quite clear as to who and what John Jones is. This is one of the great arguments of the twentieth century. Is man an animal? Is he a mechanism? Or is he more than either or both of them? Obviously Christians, who believe that God made man "in his own image,"[8] must consistently maintain that he is more than an animal, and certainly more than a machine. But we need to ask, in what way is he more?

There are many things that distinguish man from the animals, and it may be worthwhile to list some of them. Man uses tools, man uses language and other communication devices, man expresses himself in art and music, man has a religious instinct, man is conscious of his own being, man can rise above his instincts, man is aware of his own mortality, man has a moral sense and deals in the realm of such abstract concepts as beauty, justice, love, forgiveness, compassion, sympathy, generosity and kindness. Man, in short, is *personal*. He has a personality and he is a person. Without pressing those definitions, we know at heart what they mean.

Equally, of course, there are many ways in which man is linked with the animals: his senses, his appetites, his natural instincts, his physiology, his method of reproduction—all of these he shares with the animals. There is no need for Christians to be defensive here. *Homo Sapiens* is in many ways closely linked with the animals. But that is not to say that he has not another dimension.

For that matter, man has many of the qualities of an efficient machine: His skeletal and muscle systems are perfect examples of engineering, his brain is a superb computer, his eyes are the finest cameras yet devised. But he is more than a machine.

And the "plus" is the personal, the thing that not only distinguishes a man from a machine or an animal, but even distinguishes man from man. All of those personal attributes—art, music, abstract concepts, self-awareness—are distinctive to man among other creatures. And these qualities, unlike his "animal" body, are manifestly enduring. Beethoven dies, but the Ninth Symphony plays on. John Jones dies, but the love and generosity and kindness, the human interaction in which he shared, live on. There can be no doubt, at this level at least, that "something" survives death, and the something that does is linked with the element of personality rather than the body.

So far few would disagree. But all of that falls

far short of the Christian belief, which is that *personality* survives death: not just elements of it, nor memories of it, but the real person. The true John Jones—quite distinctive from Robert Brown—cannot die, and does not die. And, once again, we shall be returning to that subject later on.

What needs to be established at this stage is that man—the whole human being—is a personality in a bodily form, but that the bodily form is not the personality. True, John Jones has red hair and blue eyes—but look at that verb! He "has" them. They "belong" to him. But they, and all the other parts of his physical body, do not add up to a "person." We should never describe his personality in those terms. The real John Jones, the one who loves his wife and enjoys hiking and growing roses, is so much more than a computer linked to a machine. He is a person, and that is another way of saying he is a "soul." And it is the *person* of John Jones that survives his death, not as a fleeting spirit or emanation, but as a man.

There is quite an argument in the scientific realm, as I have indicated, between those who believe that brain is mind, and those who believe that mind uses brain. Accept the second concept, and it becomes completely rational to go on and say that mind survives the death of the brain—provided it can have a new "vehicle" for its activity. Personality is clearly connected more with the mind than the body (though it may be hard for us to conceive of personality *without* a body—as in the

Christian doctrine of God, for example), and if mind survives death there is very little difficulty in accepting that personality survives death, too.

The question then becomes, in what form does the personality of John Jones express itself after death? Professor D. M. Mackay of Keele University is one of Britain's foremost experts in the communications systems of the human brain. He also believes, as a Christian, in immortality. Here is how he sees it: "It is not as disembodied spirits that God promises us eternal life, but as personalities expressed in a new kind of body—what the apostle Paul calls a 'spiritual body.' Just as a message is still the same message, whether it's spoken in words or flashed in morse code, so, according to the Bible, we shall be the same persons, whatever the material form in which our personalities may be expressed. Nothing"—he adds—"in the scientific picture of man, however complete it may one day become, could affect the truth of this doctrine one way or the other."[9]

He sees personality as a *message*, and our present bodies as one means of transmitting that message. But like all Christians he looks ahead to a new kind of body—a better transmitter—in a new kind of life beyond death.

This is precisely what the Bible itself teaches and, as Professor Mackay so trenchantly asserts, there is nothing science can say against it. It is not intrinsically irrational, as some would claim; nor, of course, can it be rationally proved as some would wish. One can only assert that the survival of personality is what Christianity teaches, that this personality expresses itself in the "life beyond" in a new form suited to its new environment; and that this doctrine fits the available facts and answers the ultimate questions as well as, and probably a great deal better than, any theory man has yet devised.

So, where have we arrived? I conclude that, when I die, my body disintegrates, but my personality—the real me—lives on; this personality is going to express itself in the "life beyond" in a totally different kind of body. That, I have said, is the Christian position. In following chapters I shall try to justify that assertion; and then, in rather more detail, attempt to answer the question, "What kind of a 'totally different' body?" But first I would like to consider the whole question of the survival of the personality after death.

notes

[1] *SCM Press.*

[2] *In a lecture reported in* The Times, *December 12, 1967.*

[3] *Ecclesiastes 12:7.*

[4] *Arnold Toynbee, in* Man's Concern with Death, *Hodder.*

[5] *Job 19:25–27.* (King James Version)

[6] *Genesis 2:7.*

[7] *Psalm 8:5.*

[8] *Genesis 1:27.*

[9] *In an essay in* Inter-Varsity, *1970.*

3

EVIDENCES FOR SURVIVAL

The evidence *against* survival is simply expressed: it is the evidence of our own senses. When a person dies, he has gone. However we express it, we regard his life as ended. We talk about the "departed"—or used to. Not only that, but we are familiar with death in so many other realms too. Plants, fish, and animals die, and in every case death is the end. We may preserve their form but the life is gone.

In the nature of things, therefore, the evidence for survival is not so simply expressed. It has to overcome the apparently overwhelming evidence of our senses. And to introduce into it a concept which distinguishes between body and personality is to make the issue even more difficult.

Yet the fact is that the evidence *for* survival is very strong. So strong that Dr. John Beloff writing in *The Humanist* magazine in 1965 argued very persuasively that, rather than try to deny survival, humanists should accept that it probably occurs and look for a more rational explanation than that offered by religion. He suggested a theory based on the electrical impulses or waves produced by the human brain, which might continue functioning for some time—years perhaps—after death. But the point is that he felt a new theory necessary to explain a phenomenon which he accepted as undeniable, and which might "one day present a challenge to Humanism as profound in its own way as that which Darwinian Evolution did to Christianity a century ago." The evidence for the paranormal argues, he wrote, for a "dualistic world where mind or spirit has an existence separate from the world of material things." Humanists "cannot afford to close our minds . . . to the possibility of some kind of survival whether in a discarnate or reincarnate form."

What is this evidence for survival, and where does it come from? Those who suppose that it springs mainly from ghost stories and spiritualistic seances are rather out of date. The last century, (especially since the foundation of the Society for Psychical Research) has seen the amassing of an enormous amount of carefully documented evidence on the subject. It does not follow that all of this evidence is equally relevant, and some of it may even be misleading, but it cannot be ignored. Contrary to popular opinion, the SPR is not concerned solely with so-called spiritualistic phenomena; its members include people who are agnostic about survival, as well as some who are convinced supernaturalists. Its responsibility has been to investigate in a scientific and controlled way any and all psychic manifestations, and over a period of years it has documented a vast amount of material relating to death and life after death.

Spiritualism and other paranormal experiences

Let me say right away that very clearly a good deal of what is called "spiritualism" is fraudulent, or based on a combination of wishful thinking and hallucination and/or communication with evil spirits who impersonate departed human beings. Let me also say that I am convinced that the practice of attempting to communicate with the dead through mediums is wrong and harmful, and is specifically forbidden in the Bible.[1] But, whatever the motivation and however undesirable the means, there undoubtedly exists a body of well-documented phenomena associated with spiritualism which strongly suggests that human personality is not always extinguished at death.

Some years ago I met a young man who had recently become a Christian. Edward Atkinson had for twelve years previously been a convinced and active spiritualist, and one of the founders of the Young Spiritualist Council. His conversion was a painful and costly affair. He had frequently and publicly attacked Christianity, and on one fateful day, in his own words, "scornfully challenged the miserable carpenter who called himself God to invade, crush and re-make *me*." God answered the challenge. In November 1961 Edward Atkinson left the spiritualist movement. But the faculty of clairvoyance only left him fifteen months later, and he was in the intervening period the subject of constant attack by destructive spirits. Eventually, overcome by the reality of Christ in his life, they left him, and with them went his malign gift of clairvoyance.

The significance of his story is this. Although he has spent much of his time subsequently warning Christians of the dangers of spiritualism, Edward Atkinson never had any doubts at all about the reality of his earlier spiritualistic experiences or that he had in fact communicated with the discarnate spirits of the dead.[2]

The shadowy world of the spirits, from which discarnate voices bring messages to their loved ones on earth, is far removed from the heaven described by the Bible. I do not profess to know why some people after death seem able to communicate with living people through mediums, but I do not envy either them or the recipients of their messages. There is a better thing than this beyond the grave—but even saying that does not silence the testimony of these spirits to the reality of survival.

However, it is not the testimony of spiritualism with which I am concerned, except as an incidental factor. The SPR has also documented many other far more revealing and convincing incidents relating to death and the human personality. One of them is so relevant to this argument, and so well documented, that I shall reproduce it in full.[3] The late Lord Geddes wrote:

On Saturday, November 9th, a few minutes after midnight, I began to feel very ill and by 2 o'clock was definitely suffering from acute gastro-enteritis. . . . By 10 o'clock I had developed all the symptoms of very acute poisoning . . . pulse and respirations being quite impossible to count. I realized I was very ill and very quickly reviewed my whole financial position . . . thereafter at no time did my consciousness appear to me to be in any way dimmed, but suddenly realised that *my* consciousness was separating from another consciousness which was also me. These for purposes of description we could call the A and B consciousness, and throughout what follows the ego attached itself to the A consciousness. The B personality I recognized as belonging to the body, and as my physical condition grew worse . . . I realised that [it] was beginning to show signs of being composite, that is, built up of "consciousness" from the head, heart, viscera, etc. The components became more individual and the B consciousness began to disintegrate, while the A consciousness, which was now me, seemed to be altogether outside the body, which it could see. Gradually I realised that I could see not only my body and the bed in which it was, but everything in the whole house and garden, and

then I realised that I was not only seeing
"things" at home, but in London and in Scot-
land, in fact wherever my attention was di-
rected it seemed to me; and the explanation I
received, from what source I do not know, but
which I found myself calling my mentor, was
that I was free in a time dimension of space,
wherein "now" was in some way equivalent to
"here" in the ordinary three dimensional world,
but also "things" in these four and more dimensional places that I was in. From now on the
description is and must be entirely metaphorical because there are no words which really
describe what I saw or rather appreciated. Although I had no body I had what appeared to
be perfect two-eyed vision, and what I saw can
only be described in this way, that I was conscious of a psychic stream flowing with life
through time, and this gave me the impression
of being visible, and it seemed to me to have a
particularly intense iridescence. I understood
from my mentor that all our brains are just
endorgans projecting as it were from the three
dimensional universe into the psychic stream
and flowing with it into the fourth and fifth
dimensions. Around each brain, as I saw it,
there seemed to be what I can only describe in
ordinary words as a condensation of the psychic stream . . . I saw A enter the bedroom. I
realized she got a terrible shock and I saw her
hurry to the telephone; I saw my doctor leave

his patients and come very quickly, and heard him say, or saw him think, "He is nearly gone." I heard him quite clearly speaking to me on the bed, but I was not in touch with the body and could not answer him. I was really cross when he took a syringe and rapidly injected my body with something, which I afterwards learned was camphor. As the heart began to beat more strongly I was drawn back and I was intensely annoyed because I was so interested and just beginning to understand where I was and what I was "seeing". . . . Once I was back all the clarity of vision of anything and everything disappeared and I was just possessed of a glimmer of consciousness which was suffused with pain.

It is surprising to note that this dream, vision or experience has shown no tendency to fade like a dream would fade, nor has it shown any tendency that I am aware of to grow or to rationalise itself as a dream would do. I think that the whole thing simply means that but for medical treatment of a peculiarly prompt and vigorous kind I was dead to the three dimensional universe. If this is so and if in fact the experience of liberation of consciousness in the fourth dimensional universe is not imagination, it is a most important matter to place on record. . . .

This account is only one of a number which have the same characteristics—a division, in the face of death, between body and "personality."

This division is very vivid to those who reported it, though not at all terrifying or disturbing. Generally they record their reluctance to return to their bodies and re-enter "normal" life.

I do not know how much weight one should attach to this kind of thing. It is not "scientific" evidence, of course, as it is a non-verifiable record of an individual's private, interior experiences. However, when many sane and balanced people, over a long period of time but in roughly similar circumstances, record substantially the same experience, one must attach some weight to it. Certainly Lord Geddes, a very distinguished physician and professor of anatomy, would not seem to be the kind of person to indulge in fanciful make-believe about so important a topic.

A mountaineer has recorded a rather similar experience, not during the crisis of an illness, but during the few moments when he slipped over the edge of a precipice, hung some twenty feet over the edge on the end of a rope, and faced sudden death. His account is less scientific, but just as interesting.[4]

I found myself hanging on the rope a few feet below the crest of the ridge. I turned, snatched at the rocks and clawed my way back. I had fallen altogether about 20 feet and the rope . . . had held . . .

During the time I was doing this a curious rigidity or tension gripped my whole being, mental and physical . . . It was an overwhelming sensation and quite outside my experience. It was as though all life's forces were in process of undergoing some fundamental evolutionary change, the change called death . . . I know now that death is not to be feared, it is a supreme experience, the climax, not the anti-climax of life.

For how long I experienced this crescendo of power I cannot say, time no longer existed as time . . . Then suddenly this feeling was superseded by a feeling of complete indifference and detachment, detachment as to what was happening or likely to happen to that body. I seemed to stand aside from my body. I was not falling for the reason that I was not in a dimension where it was possible to fall. I, that is, my consciousness, was apart from my body and not in the least concerned with what was befalling it.

Commenting on this experience, the author says, "It is not within my province to discuss that which only death can prove; yet to me this experience was a convincing one, it convinced me that consciousness survives beyond the grave."

Two further instances, both well documented and with all the marks of authenticity, seem to support that conclusion. The first is from the First World War, and concerns an apparition reported *before* the percipient knew of his friend's death.

The percipient was Lieut. J. J. Larkin, of the R.A.F. and the apparition was that of one of

Lieut. Larkin's fellow officers, Lieut. David M'Connel, killed in an airplane crash on December 7th, 1918. Lieut. Larkin reported that he spent the afternoon of December 7th in his room at the barracks. He sat in front of the fire reading and writing and was wide awake all the time. At about 3:30 p.m. he heard someone walking up the passage.

"The door opened with the usual noise and clatter which David always made: I heard his 'Hello boy!' and I turned half round in my chair and saw him standing in the doorway, half in and half out of the room holding the door knob in his hand. He was dressed in his full flying clothes, but wearing his naval cap, there being nothing unusual in his appearance . . . I remarked 'Hello! back already?' He replied, 'Yes, got there all right, had a good trip' . . . I was looking at him at the time he was speaking. He said, 'Well, Cheerio!,' closed the door noisily and went out."

Shortly after this a friend dropped in to see Lieut. Larkin and Larkin told him that he had just seen and talked to Lieut. M'Connel. [This friend sent a corroborative statement to the Society for Psychical Research.] Later on that day it was learned that Lieut. M'Connel had been instantly killed in a flying accident which occurred at about 3:25 p.m. Mistaken identity seems to be ruled out, since the light was very good in the room where the apparition appeared. Moreover, there was no other man in the barracks at the time who in any way resembled Lieut. M'Connel. It was also found that he was wearing his naval cap when he was killed, apparently an unusual circumstance. Agent and percipient had been "Very good friends, though not intimate friends in the true sense of the word."[5]

The second instance, the Chaffin Will Case, has become famous. As Rosalind Heywood remarks, "Whatever the explanation, there is *something* to be explained."

James Chaffin, a farmer in North Carolina, died in 1921 as the result of a fall, leaving a widow and two sons. In 1905 he made a will leaving his whole property to his third son, Marshall, who proved the will and himself died bout a year later, leaving a widow and a son, a minor. In June 1925 the second son, James began to have vivid dreams of his father appearing at his bedside and speaking. This vision may have been a "borderland" experience, occurring between sleeping and waking. It was more realistic than pure dreams usually are but in an experience as informative as this the distinction is of little importance.

The figure was dressed in a black overcoat which James had often seen his father wearing. [James said that] "He took hold of his overcoat this way and pulled it back and said 'You will find my will in my overcoat pocket' and then disappeared."

James went to his elder brother's house and found the coat, and inside the inner pocket, which was sewn up, a roll of paper with the words, "Read the 27th chapter of Genesis in my daddie's old Bible." James found the old Bible in a drawer in his mother's house and in the presence of witnesses found between two folded pages on which the 27th chapter of Genesis was printed, another will, dated January 16th, 1919, whereby the Testator, "after reading the 27th Chapter of Genesis," in which the supplanting of Esau by Jacob is related, divided his property equally between his four sons, and added, "You must all take care of your Mammy."

The second will, though unattested by witnesses, was valid by the law of the State . . . Before probate, however, the Testator appeared again to his son, James, saying: "Where is my old will?" and showing "considerable temper."[6]

These instances, like earlier ones, are cited in Rosalind Heywood's contribution to the symposium *Man's Concern with Death*. She quotes the views of three distinguished scholars, none of them in any way committed to a "survivalist" position.

First, the well-known American psychologist, Professor Gardner Murphy.

Where then do I stand? To this the reply is: what happens when an irresistible force strikes an immovable object? To me the evidence cannot be bypassed, nor, on the other hand, can conviction be achieved . . . Trained as a psychologist and now in my sixties, I do not actually anticipate finding myself in existence after physical death. If this is the answer the reader wants, he can have it. But if this means that in a serious philosophical argument I would plead the anti-survival case, the conclusion is erroneous. I linger because I cannot cross the stream. We need far more evidence; we need new perspectives; perhaps we need more courageous minds. (*Challenge of Psychical Research,* Harper, New York, 1961.)

Next, the doyen of British psychologists, Professor Sir Cyril Burt.

The uncertainty leaves the matter open in *both* directions. On the one hand the theoretical psychologist (and that includes the para-psychologist) should, on this particular issue, preserve a strict agnosticism, pressing physicalistic interpretations as far as they will go, and, even if in the end he feels compelled to adopt the hypothesis of a surviving mind, he must remember that it is, like the ether of old, no more than a hypothesis. On the other hand, those who, from reasons of faith, metaphysics, or what they take to be personal revelation, still wish to believe in survival for themselves or those they love, need have no grounds for fearing scientific censure. Thus our verdict on the whole matter must be the same as that pronounced by Plato two thousand years ago—the reply he puts into the mouth of Socrates while waiting to drink the hemlock. "I would not positively assert that I shall join the company of those good men who have already departed from this life; but I cherish a good hope." Hope implies, not the virtual certainty of success but the possibility of success. And it is, I think, one important result of recent psychological and para-psychological investigations to have demonstrated, in the face of the confident denials of the materialists and the behaviourists, *at least the possibility* of survival in some form or other, though not necessarily in the form depicted by traditional piety or fourth century metaphysics. (In a symposium *Science & ESP*, Routledge and Kegan Paul.)

And finally, Professor C. D. Broad, sometime Knightbridge Professor of Moral Philosophy at Cambridge. He incidentally, does not hide the fact he does not want to survive.

The position as I see it is this. In the known relevant normal and abnormal facts there is nothing to suggest and much to counter-suggest the possibility of any kind of persistence of the psychical aspect of a human being after the death of his body. On the other hand, there are many quite well attested *para-normal* phenomena which strongly suggest the full-blown survival of a human personality. *Most people*

*manage to turn a blind eye to one or other of
these two relevant sets of data, but it is part of
the business of a professional philosopher to try
to envisage steadily both of them together. The
result is naturally a state of hesitation and scepticism*[7] (in the correct as opposed to the popular sense of that word). I think I may say that
for my part I should be slightly more annoyed
than surprised if I should find myself in some
sense persisting immediately after the death of
my present body. One can only wait and see, or
alternatively (which is no less likely) wait and
not see. *(Lectures on Psychical Research,* Routledge and Kegan Paul, 1962.)

The resurrection of Jesus

However, none of these pieces of evidence, nor all
of them taken together, is as full, as convincing,
and as consistent as the best-documented survival
of all time, the resurrection of Jesus. Undoubtedly
this must have extensive consideration in any book
on this subject, whatever one's personal beliefs or
convictions about Jesus Christ, if only because so
much has been placed upon it and so much depends upon it. It has been exhaustively studied,
both by protagonists and antagonists, and is rightly reckoned to be the absolute lynchpin of the
Christian position on life after death. Even the
apostle Paul saw it that way: "If Christ has not
been raised," wrote, "your faith is futile and you
are still in your sins."[8]

On the other hand, the resurrection of Christ is not typical of normal human experience. He claimed to be the Son of God. "It was not possible for him to be held" . . . by "the pangs of death," the apostle Peter told the awe-struck crowds at Pentecost.[9] In his case, the body did not disintegrate, but was instantly transformed, leaving behind an empty tomb. This is not the path ordinary humans are called to walk; or rather, this is not the pace at which we are called to walk it. In the resurrection event—and the ascension, when the body of Jesus Christ returned to heaven—events which "normally" take long periods of time are telescoped into a few days.

Yet in other ways it is entirely typical, and is clearly intended to be: "In fact Christ has been raised from the dead, the *first fruits* of those who have fallen asleep."[10] He is the beginning of a "harvest" of resurrections, and in that sense he is the pacemaker and the prototype.

So let us look at the resurrection of Christ, to see what it says, and what it does not say about the more general question of life beyond death. There are several far more exhaustive treatments of the subject, and these are recommended to those who would wish to pursue the details and tie up all the ends.[11] In my treatment I shall restrict myself to the "irreducible minimum"—what seems to me to be the heart of the matter.

Few people nowadays—and none at all who are taken seriously, I think—would deny that there

was a man called Jesus who lived in Judaea in the
early years of the first century AD. His existence is
not only attested by the Gospel writers (who
might be considered prejudiced witnesses) but also
by a number of distinguished secular or non-Christian historians—including the Roman, Tacitus, and
the Jew, Josephus. There is also an abundance of
archaeological material showing how far and how
fast Christianity—belief in this same Jesus as the
Son of God—had spread by about AD 70. In other
words, in a single life-time a man was born, lived,
died, and became the founder of a major religion
which held that he rose from the dead. This was
not a peripheral belief about Jesus, something his
followers could accept or reject as secondary. It
was their message—"Jesus and the resurrection."[12]

Let us be absolutely clear what this means.
Within the life-time of those who were eye-witnesses of the crucial events a major religion was
born, spread with amazing rapidity, and claimed
that its founder, executed by the Roman authorities, had risen from the dead. No amount of argument over details about the crucifixion and burial
of Christ can obscure this. *They* believed it—his
contemporaries and his opponents, including the
authorities who executed him, who were desperate
to disprove the Christian case but were obviously
unable to do so. Unlike us, they had access to
eye-witnesses. They could cross-examine them,
and probe the story for flaws or discrepancies.
Given the will to do so, it should not have been

difficult to demolish so incredible an argument as
that a man had risen from the dead. *And the will
existed,* yet it was not done, *because the resurrection was a fact.*

It is sometimes said that those were gullible
days, quite unlike our modern climate of thought;
that people then were predisposed to believe all
kinds of weird legends and fantasies. But this
simply will not hold water. The first century was
an age of cynicism and rationalism. The dominant
Greek school of thought, Stoicism, did not believe
in any kind of life after death. Neither did one of
the two major Jewish theological groupings, the
Sadducees. Thus there was no shortage of eloquent
and learned voices to do battle against any religion
or philosophy proposing as its central belief that a
man rose from the dead. The reaction of the Greek
Areopagus—a philosophical council—to Paul's message of resurrection is proof enough of that. They
listened to him attentively until he spoke of Jesus
being raised from the dead, but then the meeting
broke up. This was the point of no return. Far
from being gullibly disposed to accept it, they be-
haved exactly like their twentieth-century counter-
parts and mocked the very idea.[13]

So, from two assertions which are very nearly
undeniable—that Jesus of Nazareth existed as an
historical character in the first thirty or so years of
the first century AD, and that by AD 70 the Christian religion was well established in the Graeco-
Roman world—we are able to argue the strength of

the case for the resurrection of Jesus. Those who care to refute it must face these facts head on, and find an explanation for them that is easier to believe than that Jesus rose from the dead. So far nobody has done it.

Of course, the "case" for the resurrection of Jesus goes further than that. Any man who lives has to die, so it is easy to believe that Jesus died, too. And it is historically consistent that he should have been crucified under Pontius Pilate—the Roman Governor of Judaea at the time. Incidentally, we now have archaeological proof that Pilate actually existed—something earlier ages have lacked.

But on the third day after his death—the first Easter Sunday—his disciples discovered his tomb to be empty. That empty tomb is an important piece of evidence. After all, the burials of executed public agitators like Jesus are not hole-in-the-corner affairs. There had been rumors earlier that he would "rise from the dead," so obviously the authorities would take special care to see that he did not. We are told in the Gospels of guards around the tomb, and of the sealing of the sepulchre itself. But his disciples found the tomb empty, and within a few weeks were saying so publicly. Yet so far as history records, the authorities were unable to counter this remarkable claim. They did not produce the body of Jesus. They did not even produce the guards to say they had been attacked and the body stolen—though the idea was

put up at one stage. The only recorded explanation offered by the anti-Christian parties was that
this and all the miracles of Jesus were demonic in
origin.[14]

But it was not just that the disciples found the
tomb of Jesus empty. A number of them actually
saw him, alive, active, and vocal. Later *all* the disciples saw him—indeed, according to Paul, "more
than five hundred brethren"[15] Not only that, but
he adds "most of whom are still alive." That is the
statement of a man confident of the truth of his
evidence. "Look," he says in effect, "here is the
proof that Jesus rose from the dead. He was seen
at different times and places by all the twelve
apostles, and then on one occasion by five
hundred people . . . and if you don't believe me,
you can check it for yourself, because most of
them are still alive." As Paul wrote those words to
the church at Corinth, probably some time before
AD 70, he was inviting sceptics to put his claim to
the test. There were hundreds of eye-witnesses of
the resurrection. True, they were a few hundred
miles away in Judaea, but they were not inaccessi-
ble. Paul was presenting Christianity as it ought
always to be presented—as an historical religion,
rooted in certain events that actually happened at
a point in space and a point in history.

notes

1 *e.g. Leviticus 19:31; Deuteronomy 18:10-12.*

2 *His story was related by himself in* Crusade, *September, 1964.*

3 *An address by the late Lord Geddes to the Royal Medical Society in Edinburgh, 1937, quoted by Rosalind Heywood in* Man's Concern with Death, *Hodder.*

4 *F. S. Smythe,* The Spirit of the Hills, *Hodder, 1935.*

5 *Summarized by Professor Gardner Murphy in* Three Papers on the Survival Problem, *American Society for Psychical Research, 1945.*

6 *W. H. Salter,* Zoar, *or* The Evidence of Psychical Research concerning Survival, *Sidgwick and Jackson, 1961.*

7 *My italics.*

8 *1 Corinthians 15:17.*

9 *Acts 2:24.*

10 *1 Corinthians 15:20.*

11 *e.g.* The Evidence for the Resurrection *by J. N. D. Anderson, IVP.*

12 *Acts 17:18.*

13 *Acts 17:30–32.*

14 *See* Beyond the Gospels, *R. Dunkerley, Penguin.*

15 *1 Corinthians 15:6.*

4
WHAT KIND OF BODY?

What was it that these Christian eye-witnesses of Jesus' resurrection saw? It is an important question, highly relevant to our investigation of life beyond death. It is not enough to say that they saw, or met, Jesus. In what form did they see or meet him? Was he exactly the same in every way as before his death? If not, in what way had he changed?

Perhaps the simplest way to answer that is to make two lists, one noting the dissimilarities between the pre- and post-resurrection Christs, and the other describing the similarities.

Into the first list—the negative one—must go a number of pieces of eye-witness evidence which are frequently overlooked, or else seized upon to support a pre-conceived notion of the nature of Jesus after the resurrection. For example, it is undeniable that the appearance of Jesus was changed, and changed to such an extent or in such a way that even his closest friends failed to recognize

him. Mary of Magdala supposed he was "the gar-
dener"[1] on the morning of the resurrection. Two
disciples walked seven miles to Emmaus with him
that same day and did not recognize him until a
familiar mannerism connected with giving thanks
for the evening meal "opened" their eyes.[2] Less
obviously, Peter and the other disciples needed—
and received—other evidence than the evidence of
sight that it was in fact Jesus who met them during
their fishing expedition on the Sea of Tiberias.
This incident is in some ways the most revealing of
them all.[3]

After the resurrection—and apparently slightly
impatient at the delay in bringing in the kingdom
which they were expecting—seven of the disciples
took a boat out on this inland sea for a night's
fishing. Despite their professional skills, they
caught absolutely nothing. However, "just as day
was breaking" Jesus stood on the beach and called
to them. "The disciples did not know that it was
Jesus." He told them to cast their net on the star-
board side of the boat. They did, and caught an
enormous quantity of fish. John then shouted to
Peter "It's the Lord!" and Peter, typically, jumped
overboard and swam ashore to greet him. When
the others followed, they found that Jesus had
already lit a fire on the beach and they all had
breakfast together. At this point John observes,
"Now none of the disciples dared ask him, 'Who
are you?' They knew it was the Lord." Obviously
it was not the sense of sight that gave them this

knowledge, or they would not have even thought of asking "Who are you?" It was the miracle he had done, and the personality they knew so well, that convinced them that they were once again in the presence of their Lord.

But it was not simply the external appearance of Jesus that was changed. The physical properties of his body were also changed, and very radically indeed. Although he specifically denied that he was a ghost or spirit[4] (and clearly he was not, because he could be touched, and he was able to prepare and eat a meal) and although he had "flesh and bones," as the disciples could see,[5] yet he was able to enter rooms through locked doors,[6] appear in places many miles apart without apparently travelling by any recognized means, and eventually be "taken from their sight" on the Mount of the Ascension.[7] It is hardly necessary to say that none of these things is feasible for a human body, and in fact none of these things had happened to Jesus before during his earthly life. Before the resurrection his body was unquestionably that of a normal human being. If he did not eat, he got hungry. If he did not drink, he was thirsty. At night he was tired and needed to sleep. If he was cut, he bled. His long journey from Galilee to Jerusalem took weeks and there was never the slightest suggestion that he might travel it in any but a completely "normal" way.

Yet *after* the resurrection all this was changed. Quite obviously Paul was right when he claimed

that "Christ being raised from the dead will never
die again; death no longer has dominion over
him."[8] That in itself says something very remarkable about the body of Jesus after his resurrection.
All human bodies are mortal. They lie under the
"dominion" of death. Or, to put it in more usual
language, they begin to die from the moment they
are born. But this new body of Jesus was not subject either to the sudden onslaught of disease or
accident, nor to the insidious and irresistible process of growing old.

And this body was not confined within the
limits of our space-time world. It simply could not
have been composed as "ordinary" bodies are. It
may indeed have had flesh and bones, but it was
not limited by them in the way we are. Bars and
bolts could not shut it out, and death itself could
not touch it. It was undoubtedly a *real* body. Hundreds of people could not have been so mistaken,
especially when Jesus offered clear evidence of it.
But it was not an earthbound body. It was something that bore a developmental relationship to an
earthly human body, but it was not identical with
it. There was clearly a continuity of life between
the body of Jesus and the body of the resurrected
Jesus, but in the time between his death and resurrection it had undergone a very fundamental
change. That, at least, seems clear.

So much for the list of dissimilarities: the body
of Jesus after the resurrection had a different appearance and also a different form. It was like the

previous body, it had some sort of developmental relationship to it, but it was obviously not identical with it.

Now we must consider the similarities. Strangely, they all came down to one factor, but that factor is so important that it outweighs all the dissimilarities. It is simply this: Jesus before and after the resurrection was undeniably *the same person.* No matter what extraordinary changes had taken place in his bodily form, all who knew him well had no doubt at all who he was. They "knew" it was the Lord.

Let us see *how* they recognized him. Mary of Magdala recognized his voice—or, possibly, a familiar mode of address: the way he said "Mary." The two on the road to Emmaus recognized his mannerisms: the way he broke bread. The disciples by the lake recognized his characteristic activity in the way he performed the miracle of the fish. Even more than that they recognized his characteristic thoughtfulness in lighting the fire and preparing breakfast. In other words they all recognized the person, or the personality, of a man they had known well, and were so sure of his identity that they were prepared to die for that belief, as many of his early followers did.

What we must conclude in examining the resurrection of Jesus is exactly what we found in all the other evidences of survival: essentially what survived death was his personality. But in this case an earlier supposition—that this surviving personality would need a new bodily vehicle in which to express itself—becomes a fact. The personality of Jesus after his resurrection from death expressed itself in a new body, no longer subject to the limitations imposed on a space-time, earthly body. The "message" was the same—to use Professor Mackay's illustration quoted earlier—but the "transmitter" was new, and better. Not only was it better, in general terms (less confined, less limited, immortal) but it was also perfectly designed to live *on* in a spiritual environment. It was no longer really at home in this world.

The transformation of our bodies

And this is the pattern, according to the Bible, for all resurrection. Not immediately at death, as in the case of Jesus, but just as radically our bodies will be changed, and we shall enter a new environment in a form perfectly suited to life there. And it will be *us:* not our ghosts, not our "souls," but the whole personality will break through the barrier of flesh and on into a new realm of living, just as it did with Jesus. The apostle Paul puts it very dramatically:

> Lo, I tell you a mystery. We shall not all sleep, but we shall all be changed, in a moment, in the twinkling of an eye, at the last trumpet. For the trumpet will sound, and the dead will be raised imperishable, and we shall be changed. For this perishable nature must put on the imperishable, and this mortal nature must put on

immortality . . . Then shall come to pass the saying that is written: "Death is swallowed up in victory."[9]

But what is the relationship between our earthly bodies and our changed heavenly ones? Is there any link, any connection at all? And if not, how can there be any recognition of those we love in the life beyond death?

In a way, these questions have already been answered, if we accept the resurrection of Jesus as the prototype of all resurrection from death. As we have seen, there was a very real connection between the earthly body of Jesus and his risen one, but they were not identical. I have described the link as developmental, because that seemed a way of expressing the kind of unity which is involved. The second develops out of the first. It is a refinement of it, a further stage, a mutation, if we want a scientific term. But it could never work the other way. The one is incomparably "higher" and more advanced than the other. The continuity is of personality; the change involves the form in which that personality presents itself. Flesh and blood is our present form, with the limitations that that imposes. But what is to be our "form" in the life beyond this earth?

The early Christians at Corinth put precisely that question to the apostle Paul. Here is his reply, in full.[10]

But perhaps someone will ask, "How is the resurrection achieved? With what sort of body do the dead arrive?" Now that is talking without using your minds! In your own experience you know that a seed does not germinate without itself "dying." When you sow a seed you do not sow the "body" that will eventually be produced, but bare grain, for example, or one of the other seeds. God gives the seed a "body" according to his laws—a different "body" to each kind of seed.

Then again, even in this world, all flesh is not identical. There is a difference in the flesh of human beings, animals, fish and birds.

There are bodies which exist in this world, and bodies which exist in the heavens. These bodies are not, as it were, in competition; the splendor of an earthly body is quite a different thing from the splendor of a heavenly body. The sun, the moon and the stars all have their own particular splendor, while among the stars themselves there are different kinds of splendor.

There are illustrations here of the raising of the dead. The body is "sown" in corruption; it is raised beyond the reach of corruption. It is "sown" in dishonor; it is raised in splendor. It is sown in weakness; it is raised in power. It is sown a natural body; it is raised a spiritual body. As there is a natural body so will there be a spiritual body.

It is written, moreover, that:

The first man Adam became a living soul. So

the last Adam is a life-giving Spirit. But we should notice that the order is "natural" first and then "spiritual." The first man came out of the earth, a material creature. The second man came from heaven and was the Lord himself. For the life of this world men are made like the material man; but for the life that is to come they are made like the one from heaven. So that just as we have been made like the material pattern, so we shall be made like the heavenly pattern. For I assure you, my brothers, it is utterly impossible for flesh and blood to possess the kingdom of God. The transitory could never possess the everlasting.

The dead and the living will be fitted for immortality.

Listen, and I will tell you a secret. We shall not all die, but suddenly, in the twinkling of an eye, every one of us will be changed as the trumpet sounds! The trumpet will sound and the dead shall be raised beyond the reach of corruption, and we who are still alive shall suddenly be utterly changed. For this perishable nature of ours must be wrapped in imperishability . . .

This statement repays close study, because in it Paul expresses the heart of the Christian (as compared to the pagan) doctrine of immortality. Here is no crude idea of dead bodies rising from their graves or miraculously re-assembling after cremation, but a profound picture of development from a simpler to a more complex form of life. Paul is quite clear that our earthly bodies die. They are "perishable," with all that that implies. Those who ridicule the whole idea of resurrection must accept in fairness that Christianity has never taught that a dead human body is anything other than perishable. If they wish to attack the doctrine, let them at least pay it the minimum compliment of getting it right first. Bodies die and disintegrate, and that is that, so far as the body is concerned. "What you sow does not come to life unless it dies," says Paul, describing what happens when a seed is planted. When the plant has fully grown, what has become of the seed itself? It has gone, disappeared—its "life" now part of a greater, more complex being, its "body" utterly disintegrated. And that, he argues, is what happens to our bodies at death.

He goes further. There is to be a change of *kind.* For that he uses two analogies. The first is of different kinds of "flesh"—earthly bodies. "Not all flesh is alike," he argues. "There is one kind for men, another for animals, another for birds and another for fish."[11]

In the strictly biological sense there is not a great deal of difference between one flesh and another. Body tissue, after all, is body tissue. But Paul was not using the word in the biological sense. "Flesh" in the Bible is either the lower side of human nature or—as here—simply the bodily form of an earthly creature. There is a difference between the forms of men, animals, birds, and fish, but it is a difference within limits. They have life in common, and much more: senses, appetites, animation. But within a circle of comparability they are yet distinctively different. So—he clearly implies—is life after death from life before death.

Spiritual life is better

His second analogy is a rather obscure one to modern eyes. "There are celestial bodies and there are terrestrial bodies; but the glory of the celestial is one, and the glory of the terrestrial is another. There is one glory of the sun, and another glory of the moon, and another glory of the stars; for star differs from star in glory."[12] It is tempting to read into this passage more than it can bear. All Paul is saying, it seems to me, is that once again, within the created order, there are differences within circles of comparability. Obviously the moon *is* different from the sun, and the sun is from the earth, and one star from another. But they are all bodies in space, "heavenly bodies." It is also very probable that, using the cosmology of his day, which saw the stars and planets in a sort of hierarchical order, he was also saying that within this limited similarity there was an ascending order of "glory" from the lowest to the mightiest.

All of this leads to his positive statement that spiritual (or heavenly) life is like physical (or earthly) human life, but is more "glorious." Earthly life is perishable, crude, weak; heavenly life is imperishable, glorious, powerful. Yet there is a circle of comparability. They are not really two different things, but one is an extension or development of the other. "But it is not the spiritual which is first but the physical, and *then* the spiritual."[13] The development is not from a higher form of life to a lower one, but the opposite. There is, as we saw in the case of the risen body of Jesus, a developmental relationship between the earthly body and the resurrection body, but it is a development *upwards*. At death we move to a higher, not a lower plane of existence.

This is very important, if only because some survival theories, including re-incarnation and many kinds of spiritualism, imply the contrary. The wispy spirits who are said to blow trumpets and tap out pathetic messages from the beyond could never be described, surely, as "more glorious" than living, breathing, rational, earthly human beings? *Glory* is simply not a word one could apply to most of them or their misty world of half-reality. Equally a man re-incarnated as an animal or an insect—or even another man—could not be said to have moved upwards to a higher, more glorious mode of existence. (I realize that in most doctrines of re-incarnation there is also the opportunity to move "upwards," but only in certain circumstances.)

So the body we are to have after death (the resurrection body) is a development, a refinement of our present one, which disintegrates at death.

There is a relationship between them, but the spiritual body is infinitely "higher" and in every respect superior. The personality—the "message"—remains, but the transmitter is a much better one.

The fact is that "flesh and blood cannot inherit the kingdom of God."[14] They are excellent vehicles for the message of the human personality in space and time, but quite inadequate for it in a mode of existence where space and time are meaningless concepts. That is why this great change that Paul speaks of, this metamorphosis, has to take place. Just as the caterpillar has to be changed into the butterfly in order to "inherit" the air, so we have to be changed in order to inherit heaven. There is simply no alternative.

Let us stress again the most important fact involved here—that the spiritual body and the spiritual life are better, more glorious, more *real* than their physical predecessors. Once we really begin to think in these terms our whole attitude to death will be transformed. If all we have to look forward to at death is at best extinction, and at worst a shadowy ghost-existence in some twilight spirit world, then no wonder men face it with distaste and even fear. We do not enjoy the thought of ceasing to exist, but neither do we as normal, life-loving humans relish relegation to a kind of sub-life, which is all that most non-Christian theories of "survival" really amount to. The best of them do, it is true, look on to some kind of blissful union with "the ultimate," but none, it seems to me, can match the Christian emphasis on the superiority at every level and in every way of the life that begins at death. This is the great theme of the fifteenth chapter of Paul's first epistle to the Corinthians: the resurrection life is a life of power, achievement, splendor, beauty. It has everything good from this earthly life, but without the things that make it earth-bound, limited and frustrating. Over everything on earth hangs the dark shadow of time. We never seem to have enough of it to do all the things we should like to do, to become the people we ought to be or to get to know others as we should like to know them. And there are other limitations: pain, failing strength and sight and hearing, physical handicaps and so on. All of these detract from the quality and satisfaction of life on earth, though in overcoming the challenge of limitation men have achieved nobility and greatness, and have proved the power of God to work through human weakness.

But in the life beyond death all of these are no more. "God himself will be with them," says John in the Revelation; "He will wipe away every tear from their eyes, and death shall be no more, neither shall there be mourning nor crying nor pain any more, for the former things have passed away." [15] Yet in losing them, we do not lose what is essentially human. We do not become ghosts. We carry over all that is essential (the "kernel" as Paul put it [16]), but "God gives it a body as he has chosen."[17]

All of which emphasizes the fact that if the Christian doctrine of resurrection is true—and I have tried to show how strong and consistent it is—then there is no need for distaste or trepidation in the face of death. All that lies beyond, for those who are to be raised in Christ, is superbly good. The God who made this earth so splendid, with its wonderful variety of color and form, its joys of human love, family, and work and its magnificence of art, music, and literature, has himself promised that the *next* life will be better. What more could any doubter ask than that?

notes

[1] *John 20:15.*
[2] *Luke 24:30–31.*
[3] *John 21:1–13.*
[4] *Luke 24:38, 39.*
[5] *Luke 24:39–43.*
[6] *John 20:19.*
[7] *Acts 1:9.*
[8] *Romans 6:9.*
[9] *1 Corinthians 15:51–54.*
[10] *1 Corinthians 15:35-53 (J. B. Phillips' translation).*
[11] *1 Corinthians 15:39.*
[12] *1 Corinthians 15:40–41.*
[13] *1 Corinthians 15:46.*
[14] *1 Corinthians 15:50.*
[15] *Revelation 21:3, 4.*
[16] *1 Corinthians 15:37.*
[17] *1 Corinthians 15:38.*

WHAT IS HEAVEN LIKE?

It is not unreasonable of people to ask what Christians believe about heaven, but with the best will in the world it is not possible to find precise, clear, factual answers. The reasons for this are fairly obvious. How could you explain to a primitive tribesman what life in a modern city is like—let alone the basic principles of television, or jet travel? Yet both of us live in the same earth environment, breathe the same air, and are subject to the same physical laws. But "heaven," whatever it is, must be *fundamentally* different. It cannot be a space—time environment. It cannot—in any normal sense of the word—even be regarded as a "place." So, deprived of all those elements which enable us to describe anything in normal terms, Christians are usually reduced to saying what heaven is *like*—a device which Jesus himself used on many occasions.

So let us begin by saying what heaven is not—a very necessary exercise, since it is caricatures of the true Christian picture of heaven which have led many to reject the whole idea as childish, pre-scientific and superstitious nonsense. These caricatures have included several produced by Christian writers, including Dr. John Robinson, the former Bishop of Woolwich, in his book *Honest to God,*[1] who argued that man "come of age" could never be expected to accept the idea of heaven "up in the skies." In rejecting—rightly—the mawkish portrayals of riverside reunions above the bright blue sky favored by some Victorian hymn-writers, many people have also rejected the perfectly rational, consistent picture of heaven provided by the New Testament writers as they record the teaching of Jesus.

It simply will not do for such writers to set up these targets of straw and then solemnly (or cynically) demolish them. It is worth emphasizing that Jesus never spoke of heaven in woodenly literal terms. One should also point out that apocalyptic writings like the book of Revelation were never intended to be read as scientific accounts of factual matters and never should be. It is quite wrong to treat allegorical and metaphorical language in this unimaginative—or is it prejudiced?—way.

Heaven is not up

For example, heaven is not "up." This may come as a surprise to some readers, because if an idea is old enough, no matter how flimsy its basis, it is hard to eradicate it. A great deal of biblical language seems to support it as well: the very term "ascension"—"going up"—to describe the return of Jesus to heaven is a good example. The cosmology of the day certainly thought in terms of the earth beneath (and waters "under the earth") with the firmament above, with heaven high above all. But in a remarkable way various biblical writers at different times put the whole idea of heaven in a totally non-material, non-space—time setting. The opening of the magnificent twenty-first chapter of Revelation is an example of this: "I saw a new heaven and a new earth; for the first heaven and the first earth had passed away, and the sea was no more. And I saw the holy city, new Jerusalem, coming down out of heaven from God, prepared as a bride adorned for her husband; and I heard a great voice from the throne, saying, 'Behold, the dwelling of God is with men' . . ."[2] There is no crude materialism here. Heaven in fact comes "down," though actually all such spatial ideas are irrelevant to a place which cannot be described in terms of a space—time environment. The important thing is that heaven is where God is ("the dwelling of God is with men"), and in this new heaven God has drawn his people into a community in which he is going to dwell. In such a community God will wipe away every tear, and abolish pain, sorrow, and death . . . "for the former things are passed away."[3]

Heaven, then, is not "up" in strictly literal terms, though "up" is a good word to describe something which is superior to that which it replaces. Our normal usage of the word "higher" confirms that—higher rank, higher seniority, higher skills. In none of these cases do we literally mean "upwards" in terms of physical height, but we mean they are superior. Heaven is certainly "up" in that sense. It is infinitely "above" anything we know. But it is not up geographically—after all, what is up in Australia is down in Europe. It is different, it is not material, it is greatly superior to and more glorious than anything we know on earth, but it is not "up there," or even "out there." To cling to that kind of idea is not only to expose our faith to the peril of being discredited by materialistic science. To postulate a heaven that is geographically "up there" is to misunderstand and distort Scripture. We are not defending some dark or hidden corner of the universe where we imagine heaven may be located. Heaven is not in a corner anywhere, and it will never be located by even the most powerful radio telescopes. It is simply not in their world. It is not in their dimension: up, down, or sideways.

Neither is heaven a matter of golden streets and harps. In the terms of their day, these were symbols which simply represented the ultimate in beauty and enjoyment. Modern British people might speak of a land of endless sunshine and music, without meaning anything more than perfect holiday haunt. Heaven is no more literally made of gold and precious stones than the promised land of Canaan literally flowed with milk and honey, but the image being presented is clear enough in both cases.

Heaven for ever and ever?

The other prevailing fallacy about heaven concerns the whole question of duration. Many people have said to me that they would sooner be annihilated at the time of their death than spend eternity "playing harps." There is something decidedly un-attractive to human minds about the idea of any-thing going on for ever and ever. "I'd be bored stiff" people say. "After a few thousand years you'd have done it all . . . but there'd still be end-less time to come." They make heaven sound like a wet weekend in Peoria.

In fact, as I have tried to show, time as well as space is quite irrelevant to heaven. Just as heaven has no location in space—it can't be placed on any map of the universe—neither has it any location in chronology. It is not "in" time, and the whole idea of computing years (or any other dimension of time) in heaven is like trying to measure laughter with a ruler. It simply will not submit to that kind of description.

Heaven is where God is, we said earlier in regard to its "place." And heaven is *when* God is, too. God is everlasting. That is not the same thing as saying God lasts for ever. He has no beginning and no end. He is Yahveh (his Hebrew name), which means "I Am"—the permanently present tense.

God *exists*. He is without reference to years on a calendar. Man will be, is, and was, according to whether he is to live in the future, or live in the present, or lived in the past. God *is*. He was never younger than he is now, and he does not grow old. And that is what heaven is like. There will be no tenses there.

In passing, those who ridicule the very idea of God as eternal, without beginning or end, might care to reflect on the alternative possibilities. If there was a time when God did not exist, then he "came into existence" and is a dependent being like we are. If there is to be a time when God ceases to exist then he is as subject to mortality as we are. By definition, God is self-existent, depending on no one else, and the ultimate source of being. As soon as we use the word "God" we accept that it must refer to a self-existent being. Otherwise we are simply devaluing it and evacuating it of any distinctive meaning.

Having looked at some negatives about heaven, we might now try to answer the question, what is heaven like? In fact, the negatives have themselves provided some of the answers. If heaven is not located in the dimensions of space and time, then it is an entirely different mode of existence from any we have ever known or imagined. It is literally beyond comprehension. Perhaps that is why so many modern people react negatively to heaven, or ridicule the very idea. Because it is "beyond them", in every sense, it seems unbelievable.

Clues about heaven

But the Bible does provide quite a number of helpful clues to what heaven is like. We have mentioned two: heaven is *where* God is, *when* God is. Heaven is being with God (and hell, we might add, is being where God is not: an appalling concept).[4] So heaven is in many respects "like" God, replete with beauty, truth, and goodness, eternal and personal. But it is not just a series of abstract qualities. It is a mode of *living,* where relationships are important and where we can all develop a greater insight into truth and experience love as never before. "Love never ends." says Paul, with deep satisfaction. "Now I know in part; then I shall understand fully."[5]

The heavens of materialistic religions (such as the *Valhalla* of the Norsemen or the Elysian fields of the Romans) are really little more than glamorized recreations of life on earth. At the other extreme, the heaven of the Eastern religions, like *nirvana,* are little more than concepts—they hardly involve "living," in any ordinary sense of the word. But the Christian heaven avoids both extremes. It is no mere second inning of earthly existence, improved mainly by the absence of certain serious handicaps, such as pain and death; but neither is it simply a concept. In heaven we will live, and live more fully and satisfyingly than ever before. And that life will involve all the really important elements of what we know as life: relationships, development, knowledge, communication . . . and all in the same mode as life on earth: personality expressed through a body. The differences are enormous, but do not diminish in any way the quality of life. We shall recognize our loved ones, but more by who they *are* than by what they look like. But better than that, we shall know them with a depth and insight and love unimaginable in our present human existence. Life will be transformed in the presence of its creator and sustainer.

In the light of this wonderful picture, painted for us by the biblical authors and by Jesus Christ himself, many of the most common questions about heaven can be seen in their true light, as misconceptions or irrelevancies. Will there be animals in heaven? Shall we speak English (or German, or Italian, or whatever)? What age will we be in heaven? How can anywhere be large enough to contain all the people who have ever lived and died? And so on. The answer to them all is really the same. Because heaven cannot be distorted into our space—time terms, there are simply no words or pictures that can convey its properties to space—time minds. This may seem inadequate, but it is the truth. If there is a heaven at all, then by definition it must be almost beyond our comprehension.

Yet it is linked with this life. That is important. It develops out of it. Human personality flowers there into its finest and most wonderful form, which is in fact the personality of Christ. This is how the apostle John put it: "We are God's children now; it does not yet appear what we shall be, but we know that when he appears we shall be like him, for we shall see him as he is."[6] That is man's destiny in heaven—to be like Christ: not Christ limited, as he was on earth, to the confines of time and flesh, but Christ risen, the great, free, timeless Christ of Easter morning. That, in a sentence, is what we shall be like in heaven; and a community of people like that is what heaven will be.

notes

[1] *SCM Press, 1963.*
[2] *Revelation 21:1–3.*
[3] *Revelation 21:4.*
[4] *2 Thessalonians 1:9.*
[5] *1 Corinthians 13:8, 12.*
[6] *1 John 3:2.*

WHO GOES THERE?

There is one question which is fundamental to this whole discussion but which I have carefully avoided until now. Granted that there is a heaven to which it is possible to go after death, *who* goes there? Everybody? Or just some people? And if only some, on what grounds is the selection made? Obviously these questions have been raised over and over again, throughout human history. Surprisingly, almost all known religions have settled for what is, on the face of it, the less attractive notion: that heaven is by selection, and that the selection is on grounds of moral excellence.

There could be many reasons for this. The existence of a judgment after death whose results would justly determine one's eternal destiny is a powerful incentive to obedience on earth. So selection has provided religious leaders with a very powerful and effective sanction on their followers. "Do what we say, and you will go to heaven. Disobey, and your destiny will be destruction" . . . or whatever brand of hell the particular religion promoted.

Equally the need to attain certain moral, ethical, or heroic standards to gain entrance to heaven has spurred people on to greater effort and self-discipline. It has also, at times, spurred them to extreme generosity and filled the temple coffers of many an unscrupulous high priest.

Yet the fact remains that such a remarkable preponderance of opinion in favor of a "selectional" system is strong *prima facie* evidence for an element of truth, or at any rate of psychological need. If an idea is persistent throughout human history, and right around the world (like the flood myths, for instance, or the idea of sacrifice in worship) then one must assume that it has some roots in reality, at one level or another. And this idea of a division in mankind at death, between those who merit heaven and those who deserve hell is quite surprisingly persistent. There are religions which preach universalism, of course—that all men will end up in heaven, whatever their behavior on earth—but they are exceptional.

There is one very strong rational, philosophical argument for the idea of judgment after death which I find highly persuasive. It depends upon this basic premise: that there is a God and that he is good. If that idea is rejected then there is plainly no reason for believing in any kind of moral judgment after death. But if it is accepted, then the logic of the case is almost irresistible. This life is manifestly unjust. The good suffer, the unselfish are exploited, the meek are terrorized, the poor are deprived. Conversely, the evil flourish, the selfish make fortunes, the brutal oppress the meek, and the rich get richer. Tyrants die peacefully in their beds while saints expire in agony on the rack or the pyre. Of course there are plenty of exceptions. Possibly the evil are no happier in their circumstances than the good. But clearly there is no general justice. The most massive injustices go unpunished, and the most impressive unselfishness goes unrewarded.

The instinct of justice is very strong in all of us. "It's not fair" is one of the first things a small child learns to say. We are constantly appealing to some abstract principle of justice whose existence we assume and which we also assume is recognized by everybody else. Communists, atheists, humanists, and believers all make this same appeal: "It's not fair." And yet we all also know that, in the final analysis, this life is *not* fair. With the best intentions in the world, human justice is fallible. With the worst intentions—as with a Hitler or a Stalin, for example—injustice becomes rampant.

If—as we are assuming—there is a God who is all-powerful and good, how can he possibly allow this state of affairs to continue? If he does nothing, either now or after this life, to redress such gross injustice and put down such rampant evil, he is either not all-powerful (and so cannot do it) or he is not good (and so does not care). But if he is

all-powerful and good—which is what the word
"God" means to most of us—then it seems to me
he *must* act to put things right. Justice on a cosmic
scale must be done, and must be seen to be done,
or God is not God. Very obviously he has not yet
done this on earth. The strong presumption, then,
is that he will do it after this life is over. And so
the Bible teaches: "It is appointed for men to die
once, and after that comes judgment."[1] The
theme of the final judgment of God, in which the
mighty are put down from their thrones, the
proud are scattered in the imagination of their
hearts, the rich sent empty away and the good
who are hungry and poor are exalted, runs strongly through the teaching of Jesus and the apostles.
It might seem that God is blind to human injustice, but one day it will be seen that he cares
intensely about it, and the inequalities and evils of
life on earth will be put right.

A vital part of this process is the judgment of
the individual after death. Jesus described it in
terms of a shepherd separating the sheep from the
goats.[2] However much it may offend liberal senti-
ment, there can be no doubt at all that Jesus believed and taught that there was a very real possibility of people being excluded from heaven. The
reason for this is quite uncomplicated. Heaven (in
the Christian sense) is a community of total goodness, living in the presence of God. To allow evil
into heaven would be like tossing a bad apple into
a barrel of good ones: the place would no longer

be totally good, and soon might become totally
evil. All impurity and sin is to be excluded from
heaven, simply so that it may be heaven: "Nothing
unclean shall enter it, nor any one who practises
abomination or falsehood, but only those who are
written in the Lamb's book of life."[3]

Who can possibly qualify?

But in that case we may well ask, who can possibly
hope to enter heaven? Where is the person good
enough to live in a community of total goodness,
without spoiling it? Surely God is going to be very
lonely, sitting in the isolation of his holy beauty,
while all his fallible, grumbling, morally imperfect
creatures are excluded from this new kind of Holy
Club.

But the last phrase of that verse from Revelation gives the answer. It is those whose names are
written in the "Lamb's book of life" who enter
heaven. Who are they? The same book tells us.
They are members of a "great multitude which no
man could number, from every nation, from all
tribes and peoples and tongues . . . who have
washed their robes and made them white in the
blood of the Lamb."[4] The "Lamb" is, of course,
Jesus Christ, and the reference to his blood is to
his sacrifice of himself on the cross where he died
for the forgiveness of men's sins. Through that
sacrifice, Christians believe, it is possible for ordinary men and women, fallible and faulty as we all
are, to be forgiven and accepted by God. In the

peculiar imagery of the book of Revelation, their names are "written in the Lamb's book of life." They will go to heaven, not on their own merits, as it were, but on his, because he has died for their sins. That is the Christian gospel. It is God's way of keeping heaven holy and yet admitting to it people no better than we are.

So the short answer to the question, who goes to heaven? is—those whose sins have been forgiven through the sacrifice of Jesus Christ. But this raises several more questions.

How, for example, can a person receive this forgiveness? The answer here is very clear and straightforward. The basic message of the New Testament is just this: turn from your sins, ask God to forgive you, put your trust in Jesus Christ, and God will accept you, whoever you are.

But what about those who have never even heard of Jesus Christ? What about the countless millions who follow other religions? What about those who lived in all the long centuries before Jesus Christ was born? Rather than attempt an answer myself, I shall simply quote the apostle Paul dealing with this very question: "When the gentiles, who have no knowledge of [God's] Law, act in accordance with it by the light of nature, they show that they have a law in themselves, for they demonstrate the effect of a law operating in their own hearts. Their own consciences endorse the existence of such a law. For there is something which condemns or commends their actions. We may be sure that all this will be taken into account in the day of true judgment, when God will judge men's secret lives by Jesus Christ, as my gospel plainly states."[5]

When shall we enter heaven?

One further question remains: when shall we enter heaven? Is it immediately at death, or at some future great Day of Judgment? Whole books have been written in the past fighting over this particular controversy, with some arguing that at death we immediately pass into the presence of God, some arguing that we "sleep" until the day of resurrection, and others taking all manner of considerations of, or compromises between, these two viewpoints.

Just to make myself thoroughly unpopular with all those who enjoy the fascinating exercise of splitting theological hairs over these matters, I want to say that all such argument seems to me totally irrelevant. If, as we have seen, time is meaningless in the spiritual world, then even to discuss intervals of time or the passing of "x" centuries or "y" aeons before or after the resurrection seem a singularly futile exercise. The Bible itself is quite clear about this, really: a day in God's sight is as a thousand years, and a thousand years is as a day.[6] The time taken for the metamorphosis between the physical and the spiritual world is given by Paul as "the twinkling of an eye."[7] When Christ returns to earth, as the Bible teaches he will, to inaugurate the final judgment of mankind, those who are alive at the time will "not precede those who have fallen asleep."[8] All will be raised together, in one instant of time and with no conscious elapsing of time between their individual moments of death and the moment of resurrection. And at that moment we shall enter heaven.

Yet, in fact, "enter" is the wrong word. As we have seen, heaven is not a place, in the geographical sense, but a mode of existence, and it is entered not by any physical journey—the soul winging its way through the void of space to some distant celestial destination—but by a spiritual one. In a very real sense we can make that journey now. As Paterson Smyth wrote, "Though there is a special place which shall be Heaven, yet if Heaven means a state of mind rather than a place of residence, though it is a place of residence too, if Heaven means to be something rather than to go somewhere, though it means to go somewhere too, then the answer is easy. We enter heaven by a spiritual, not by a natural act. We begin Heaven here on earth . . . by taking a journey from a bad state of mind to a good state of mind—from that state of mind which is enmity against God to that of humble, loyal, and loving obedience to Christ. It is not so much that we have to go to Heaven. We have to do that too. But Heaven has to come to us first. Heaven has to begin in ourselves."[9] We are motivated on our journey to Heaven by the reality of Heaven's present sweetness in us.

Ready for death

And it can begin now. Eternal life is something that can invade physical life, seeping back into the life lived on earth from the life to be lived in heaven. That is how the great saints and mystics have lived, *with eternity already in their hearts.* And that is the best possible preparation for the moment of death, whenever it is to come to us. Those who have begun a "life in Christ" on earth find the transition between the two worlds so easy as to be almost imperceptible. Many witnesses confirm this—of the joy and even eagerness with which those who have lived close to God on earth face the prospect of entering into an even closer relationship with him in heaven. As Paul puts it, "For to me to live is Christ, and to die is gain."[10] If life means being with Christ, then death must be gain because it will mean a closer relationship with him, with all the barriers of mortality and sin broken down.

Leslie Weatherhead puts into words the experience of many priests, ministers, and doctors who have watched people die. "I have seen a number of people die," he writes, "and I have made enquiries of nurses and doctors. You'll appreciate that most people die following a state of unconsciousness. Either they are in a coma or are drugged. But I have sat at the bedside of a man who was dying and conscious to the end. He gripped my hand and I must have gripped his more tightly than I thought I was doing, for he said, 'Don't hold me back. I can see through the gates. It's marvelous.'

"If you have seen, as I have, a women so ill that she couldn't life her head from the pillow, if you had seen her sit up, her eyes open with tremendous delight, and joy in her face, if you had heard her call the name of a beloved husband who had been dead twenty years, you would find it strangely convincing. People may say it was probably an hallucination, or a trick of the brain. All I can say is that it was very convincing to the onlooker that she really was in touch with the beloved dead and that he was coming back to welcome her."[11] Dr. Weatherhead claimed to have collected dozens of similar instances. Indeed, he goes so far as to claim, on the basis of his enquiries made over a long period of time, that "never once has anybody died in mental unhappiness." Death is "an extremely happy experience." He even quotes a physician to the royal family who said when he was dying, "If I had the strength to hold a pen I would tell mankind what a wonderful thing it is to die."

Whether or not this is true for people in general, surely for those who can look to meeting a God they have loved for many years but never seen, death will be a great joy. It is all a question of perspective. Most of us may well fear the idea of dying. But for those whose trust is in Christ there can be no basis for fear at the thought of death. The only people who rationally may fear death are those who know that God exists, and yet have lived their lives as though he did not.

We began this book by looking at the way modern man regards death: fascinated by it, yet repelled, because it strikes at the roots of his self-sufficiency. We end it by affirming that for modern man, as for all men everywhere and in every age, death is not the end. It is not the end of life, or love, or beauty. It is not the end of anything good, worthwhile, or lovely. It is not the end of those we love, nor is it the end of our own spiritual and moral development. Like sailors looking out over the water, we can only see as far as the horizon that men call death. But beyond that horizon lies more, so much more; hidden from our eyes, but revealed, item by item, to our minds and our hearts by faith, and through the words of Jesus. Evil, not death, is the final enemy of man. Death is the final enemy of man's final enemy. Beyond it lies a new kind of life, where evil has no place at all.

notes

[1] *Hebrews 9:27.*
[2] *Matthew 25:31, 32.*
[3] *Revelation 21:27.*
[4] *Revelation 7:9, 14.*
[5] *Romans 2:14–16 (J. B. Phillips' translation).*
[6] *2 Peter 3:8.*
[7] *1 Corinthians 15:52.*
[8] *1 Thessalonians 4:15.*
[9] The Gospel of the Hereafter, *Hodder.*
[10] *Philippians 1:21.*
[11] Life Begins at Death, *Denholm House Press.*

The Christian Book Promotion Trust has been formed to aid in the promotion and distribution of books which will speak significantly to the deep spiritual needs of our day, needs which the Trust believes to be as real as the more obvious physical, emotional and educational areas of human deprivation.

Among the spiritual needs they seek to alleviate are those of the bereaved and those who fear death. Hence their support of this book with its clear and confident restatement of the grounds of the Christian's hope of eternal life.

Why is such a Trust needed? Unfortunately, the economics of publishing do not always allow for an extensive advertising and promotion program, even for the most deserving of books. So the Christian Book Promotion Trust (non-profit) provides additional funds and advertising to make books such as this more widely-known and available.

This program is possible on a substantial scale only through voluntary donations. Contributions or requests for further information may be sent to:

THE CHRISTIAN BOOK PROMOTION TRUST
388 Woodstock Road, Oxford, England
North American residents may direct mail to:
THE CHRISTIAN BOOK PROMOTION TRUST
Box 567, Wheaton, Illinois 60187